I'M SO TIRED OF OTHER PEOPLE, I'M DATING MYSELF

I'M SO TIRED OF OTHER PEOPLE, I'M DATING MYSELF

An Insider's Guide to Being Single

MICHAEL NOLAN & EVE SARRETT

A JANET THOMA BOOK

THOMAS NELSON PUBLISHERS
Nashville

Published in Nashville, Tennessee, by Janet Thoma Books, a division of Thomas Nelson,
Inc., Publishers, and distributed in Canada by Word Communications, Ltd., Richmond,
British Columbia, and in the United Kingdom by Word (UK), Ltd., Milton Keynes,
England.

Library of Congress Cataloging-in-Publication Data

CIP 93-85440

2 3 4 5 6 — 98 97 96 95 94 93

DEDICATION

To Joe and Mildred Nolan
who passed on the humor genes.
—Michael

To Doug, Camden, and McCall
for giving me sheer pleasure in life
and to Mom and Dad for giving Howard, Nova, and me
a memory-filled childhood.
—Eve

ACKNOWLEDGMENTS

Thanks to all of our friends who endured our one-track minds as we tried to get a grip on singleness.

Michael would like for anyone he's dated in the past year to know that he really wasn't intending to do research when you went out.

Ones upon a time: the uncertain beginning of SINGLEHOOD

In writing this book, we wanted to gain a broad perspective of what it means to be single. So we talked to a lot of people—most of whom were only too willing to express their frustrations with the opposite sex, recount horror stories about irritating roommates, or confess their personal phobias and neuroses. We are extremely grateful for their help and hope that this book will be fabulously successful so that we can give them gift certificates for counseling next Christmas.

What does it mean to be "single"? And when is one considered "single"?

For some, being single means freedom to call their own shots, to be spontaneous, to win the Most Popular title they failed to garner in high school. For others, being described as single is an indictment: "Have you met my undesirable friend?"

Certainly, there have been many married men who have thought of themselves as single, and their lives have been chronicled in numerous country songs. But for our purposes, a single person is anyone who has entered that awkward period of life after adolescence and remains unmarried.

Western civilization seems to treat single women less kindly than it does single men. Unmarried men gain some dignity in being called bachelors. And they are able to maintain this status until they become those cranky old guys who have hair growing out of their ears and who run kids out of their yards. Then they're labeled codgers, and it doesn't really matter if they are married or what they are called.

Women, however, have to deal with such archaic names as "spinster" and "old maid." Neither sounds like a noble calling. Instead, the terms tend to conjure images of Miss Havershim in *Great*

Expectations, Miss Gulch in *The Wizard of Oz,* or Miss Hathaway in "The Beverly Hillbillies."

Perhaps in these changing times political correctness will prevail, and new terminology will find acceptance. Perhaps you can refer to yourself as "relationally challenged" or "matrimonially impaired."

On second thought, maybe it's not so bad to be "single" after all.

Link your hopes for relationships to a CHAIN LETTER

Dear Single Friend,

Are you spending your Saturday nights cleaning your house instead of painting the town? Are the only kisses you get coming from a bag of Hersheys chocolates? Are you at a point in life where you are willing to try anything to meet new people?

Then, allow me to demonstrate the amazing power of this singles chain letter. It has already gone around the world nine times and brought an end to that gross sense of alienation many people feel.

Tom R. in Nottalottaluv, Michigan, hadn't even received junk mail since 1978. Then one day, this letter arrived in his box, he responded, and today he is the beleaguered father of nine children. When Debbie L. in Trailerville, Alabama, sent out her letters, she instantly went from spending lonely nights watching television to spending her nights writing letters to her 200 plus penpals, including an entire cellblock in Parchman, Mississippi. How's that for results?

This letter, if copied and sent along to ten of your single friends, has the power to put you in touch with 352 other single people.

Here's all you have to do: Remove the name at the top of the list; add your name to the bottom; photocopy it; and send copies to ten of your friends within forty-eight hours. (No faxing—we want to maintain the personal nature of this correspondence.) Within two weeks, you should receive mail from hundreds of people at the end of their ropes—just like you. Amazing, huh?

Remember that you must take action within forty-eight hours or, well, we don't want to talk about what might happen to you. Besides you're not getting any younger. Don't break this chain or the hearts of hundreds of singles waiting to hear from you.

65% of Americans think married people are happier than single people.[1]

    That really bums out single people.

51% of never-married adults between 20 and 29 live with their parents.[2]

    It is not known how many parents have considered running away from their own homes.

22% of Americans 18 years and older have always been single.[3]

> And they'd prefer you not remind them of that, thank you.

66% of American men believe in love at first sight.[4]

> It is not known how many think love is blind.

13% of American high-school seniors never go out on a date.[5]

> Who says high school doesn't prepare you for the real world!

70% of American women will marry at least once.[6]

> The other 30% will be really hacked about having a closet full of old bridesmaids' gowns.

55% of women are likely to find romance on the job.[7]

> It happened all the time on "L.A. Law."

57% of American women believe in love at first sight.[8]

> Although there is no reason to assume there is any correlation, 57% of American women are very afraid of snakes.[9]

Only 3% of Americans think the word *risk* usually describes something good.[10]

 And you wonder why more people aren't dating?

21% of Americans say people marry because marriage is better than living alone.[11]

 Apparently, not everyone has seen "Married . . . With Children."

39% of American fifth-graders say they are in love.[12]

 Lucky little squirts.

41% of American prisons live in single-occupancy units.[13]
Although extremely economical for the resident, this is not
generally viewed as the best way to get "a place of your own."

10% of American men feel that marriage costs them their individual
identity.[14]
It is believed that many more go through life unable to answer the
question "Who am I?"

NEW TERMS for the nineties

Pringles—Professional singles

Tingles—Touchy singles

Shingles—Unmarried roofers

Zengles—Singles who follow the teachings of Buddah

Quadringles—Four single people in one dwelling

Gringles—slang for Anglo singles in a Hispanic community

Wringles—Elderly singles

Thingles—Possessions-possessed singles

Flingles—Singles capable of only short romantic relationships

Kingles—Singles who express an undying devotion for Elvis

Sing-Singles—Unmarried men in California maximum security prison

Ba-da-bingles—Singles who tell bad jokes which they punctuate with verbal impersonations of a rimshot

Lauraingles—Unmarried women who have nothing better to do than watch "Little House on the Prairie"

Stage a multicar accident, which allows you to get names and numbers of people you might never meet otherwise.

Go to the airport arrival area and hold up a sign reading SMITH for deplaning passengers to read.

Fake losing a contact in public place.

Start sing-alongs on mass transit system.

Take extra blankets to winter football games; offer to snuggle with people in your section.

Ask for second opinions at a Christmas tree lot.

Train your dog to run to attractive strangers (it worked in *101 Dalmatians*).

Dress nicely, go to court hearings, and become a character witness for people you've never met.

Always bring additional quarters to laundromat in case someone interesting needs change.

Walk up to strangers and say, "How weird! I dreamed about you last night!"

Take a Twister board to a doctor's waiting room.

Go to a bus station and shout, "Would anyone here like to be the beneficiary of my life insurance policy?"

New reasons to explain why you're NOT MARRIED

I'm hooked on Campbell's Meals-for-One.

I have traditional non-family values.

I can't find anyone who organizes his/her music collection or kitchen the way I do.

I just don't have the energy to do the "relationship thing."

When you marry, you become boring . . . uh, not that you're boring . . . I'm speaking in generalities and you're certainly the exception to the rule.

It makes "Seinfeld" funnier.

How will your single friends get a ride to the airport if you marry?

Someone's got to live in these teeny apartments.

I just don't like the idea of getting all dressed up for a wedding.

Why would I want to ruin my decor with a houseful of crummy brass candlesticks given as wedding presents?

Bad CONVERSATION-STARTERS

Gosh, it's nice to be someplace where they don't make you take Demerol at nine o'clock.

Want to go back to my pod . . . uh, pad? I meant to say *pad*.

I spent a lot of time in prison dreaming of a woman like you.

I can see myself reflected in your eyes and I look terrific.

I'm looking for a husband who can be a strong role model for my eleven children.

You look like someone with low standards.

I just got dumped by the most wonderful girl in the world. Would you mind if I rebound with you?

You know, I was selected as a finalist in the Publishers Clearinghouse sweepstakes.

Excuse me, were you in *Quest for Fire?*

Would you be interested in co-signing a loan for me?

Being asked to bring chips or brown-and-serve rolls to potluck dinners while all married people are asked to bring real food.

Someone yelling, "Everyone grab a partner," before games or dances.

Embarrassing announcements over restaurant public address system: "Smith, party of one."

TV show "Rhoda" sure was more fun before she married Joe.

If you live alone, there's no one to give you a second opinion on whether the milk has gone bad.

When you go to a restaurant by yourself, you always get a crummy table.

Discriminatory pricing structures: Couples $25, Singles $15.

Bread gets stale before you use the whole loaf.

Can't watch baseball games because the term "sacrifice single" is a real downer.

Being asked to work longer hours than married people because "you don't have family."

Subjecting your dates to the company parties.

Discriminatory evaluation of your personal calls received at work: when a co-worker gets a call from a spouse, it's considered important; when you receive a call from a friend, it's considered a nuisance.

Bosses assume your salary requirements are lower than those of a married person.

No way to get payback for all those wedding and baby shower gifts you've bought.

Personal Ads being placed between classifieds for Therapists and Escort Services.

Busboys clear your table when you go to the bathroom.

Forced off the skating floor during Grand March and Couples Skate.

The singles CONTROVERSY
Minority status orientation vs. choice

In recent years, there has been increasing pressure to recognize singles as a minority group. According to researchers, two in ten American adults have never been married, a statistic which indicates that the single population is indeed a minority.

The issue, however, has been hotly debated between two groups of people—orientationists, or those saying they are single by nature, and freedom of choice representatives, those saying singles choose their state of being. Orientationists support singles gaining minority status, saying it's time singles get their due. Opponents, including many mothers of singles, say it's time for singles to stop being so career-focused, self-absorbed, and admit they're to blame for ruining their lives and keeping more wonderful grandchildren from entering the world.

The Oratory of Orientation Activists

Being single is more than just a choice—it is the natural state of things. Excluding the rare occurrences of multiple births, each of us is born single. We spend our formative years as single people. We learn to walk and talk as single people. And we do not join anyone to form a pair unless we are participating in one of those embarrassing Little Mr. and Miss pageants.

In some ancient civilizations, parents choose husbands and wives for their offspring from the birth of the child. But think about it: Where are those cultures now? They've been reduced to nice tourist attractions for American and Japanese visitors. Or their people are still running around in loincloths, thousands of miles away from the nearest automated teller machine.

To ask single people to give up what we've always known is like asking circus bears to ride bicycles. We were born single and should have the right to stay what we were by birth, a distinct sector of the populace.

Free to Choose

We are born in this world with a plethora of options: whole wheat or sourdough, mustard or mayo, cold or heated, to marry or not marry. All of these are choices. As certainly as one is not born to be a whole wheat, with mustard, cold sandwich eater, one is not born with the inclination to be either single or married.

Dysart said that we are bound by certain genetic constraints that would keep us from varying from what has always been; this is assuredly false. How else can you explain Baskin-Robbins' *Flavor of the Month?* We are clearly people of choice and, in fact, were created to choose.

Reaching back through the annals of time, we find God saying to Adam in the Garden of Eden that it was not good for man to be alone. Next thing you know, Adam saw the dawn of Eve. He could've gone running to the other side of creation and got a studio apartment but he made a choice to stay put and marry Eve (though we don't known who served as best man and bridesmaid). Granted, they made a mess of things together but that, too, was a choice.

These days many singles redirect their energies that might otherwise be spent on a mate to their employer. With this in mind, we offer these corporate wedding vows.

I, (name), take this job to be my lawfully wedded spouse. I promise to love, honor, cherish, and keep it, and to feel like this existence is confined unto me and me only. I promise to cleave to it, forsaking all others, including friends, family, and members of the opposite sex. I take this job to have and to hold me up from having a life apart from work, to cherish late at night and on most weekends. In spite of downscaling, restructuring, and takeovers, I will hang in there for better or worse, for richer or poorer, in sickness and in health till someone makes me a better offer.

BUMMERS of living alone

No one to blame when the answering machine is left off.

Hard to get excited about great buys on twenty-pound turkeys.

All house noises are assumed to be prowlers.

Your Christmas tree seems understocked with presents.

Hanging pictures straight takes forever.

You spend an unsettling amount of time wondering how long it will take for your body to be found if you die suddenly.

Feel left out when fast food restaurants run specials on two-for-one dinner specials.

Moving furniture takes amazing ingenuity.

No one handy to help if the refrigerator falls on you.

When grisly crimes are committed in the neighborhood, everyone fingers you, the local loner, as the prime suspect.

OPENING LINES that tell you your new roommate won't work out

It's good to meet you. May I borrow $20?

You don't have anything against snakes, do you?

I hope the boys in the Federal Witness Relocation Program don't screw up again like last time.

I hate being encumbered by clothes, don't you?

My favorite movie is *Texas Chainsaw Massacre*. What's yours?

Did I mention that I'm learning to play the bagpipe?

With the incense I burn, you'll hardly notice my cigar smoke.

I hate it when landlords are really picky about rent being in on time.

Do any of your neighbors have expensive stereos?

I'm kind of a nightowl. That's when aliens usually like to make contact.

When you see how tiny Fuzzy is, you'll hardly believe she could be nursing seven kittens.

Don't you hate it when those voices inside your head chant, "Kill! Kill! Kill!"

Tip No. 1 The fastest way to rid your tub of unsightly soap scum is to pull the shower curtain.

Tip No. 2 To avoid the embarrassment of people detecting dust accumulation on furniture, use 20-watt bulbs in all light fixtures.

Tip No. 3 If you feel compelled to redecorate, never move large pieces of furniture, such as sofas or bookcases. If you do, you will inevitably find a treasure trove of food remnants, fully-grown dust bunnies, and other archaelogical items which may force you into vacuuming.

Tip No. 4 To save on kitchen clean-up, eat your foods from the container you use to cook them.

Tip No. 5 Vacuum pants to pick up light dirt, cigarette ashes, and crumbs. It's faster and cheaper than doing laundry, plus it makes ironing unnecessary.

Tip No. 6 Crumbs in the bottom of toaster make excellent micro-croutons.

Tip No. 7 Make sure the floor of your closet is large enough to contain all the clothes you own.

Tip No. 8 Wear as little clothing as possible each day—this decreases your laundry load.

Tip No. 9 White marble sinks make it almost impossible to detect splotches of toothpaste scum.

Tip No. 10 Choose bathroom carpeting that matches your hair color.

Democracy

Instituted when too many nice people gather under one roof. Always afraid of offending each other, decisions are made through a never-ending ping-pong conversation, which alternates from "I don't care. What do you think?" to "Really, it doesn't matter to me," reminiscent of a "Chip and Dale" cartoon.

Socialism

Founded on the principle of shared resources, the motto of "Whatever's yours is mine" is lived out. Translated into user-friendly terms, this becomes "If the shoes fit, I'll wear them."

Because your belongings are technically no longer yours in the socialist house, you must add five to ten minutes to each changing of clothes so you can retrieve desired items from the closets, dressers, or clothes baskets where they may have roamed.

Dictatorship

This house is run with an iron hand by whoever gets his/her name on the lease or mortgage; other roommates must bow to the throne. All acts of defiance, structural modification of the dwelling, and alteration of established policies are sternly met with the response, "Of course, that doesn't matter to you. It's not your name that's on the dotted line."

Feudal lordship

Grateful to have a satisfactory place to take shelter from the elements, the inhabitants of this household live in quiet coexistence with the one who found the domicile in the first place and offered the misplaced peasants a good deal at an opportune time.

Monarchy

Functioning as a dictator in exile, the monarch lives by himself/herself to avoid confrontations. Aside from experiencing mild panic attacks over strange creaking noises in the night, the monarch doesn't have to worry about responding to anything.

All those sequined jumpsuits in the closet (they can't be just for costume parties).

Says "thanyavarymush" when complimented.

Traded sub-compact for El Dorado.

Hums theme from *2001* before entering a room.

Kicked hole in bedroom wall practicing karate.

Seems just a little too good at pelvic tilt in aerobics class.

Seen trying to turn hubcap into belt buckle.

Numerous long distance calls traced to *National Enquirer*.

Find fried-banana-and-peanut-butter sandwiches hidden around apartment.

Makes frequent pilgrimages to Michigan Burger Kings.

Says rhinestones on glasses make them easier to find in the dark.

Seems to have an endless supply of scarves.

Sideburn-shaped chunks missing from black shag carpeting.

When you live together with several singles under one roof, you must be aware of the unspoken rules about the use of the kitchen.

If you buy your groceries separately, for example, it's okay to steal (aka borrow) from your roommates as long as they cannot detect the theft. You can scarf a cup of juice from a gallon jug as long as the container is at least one-quarter full because it will never be missed. The same rule applies to cereal boxes. Less than a quarter-stick of butter is a freebie; so is a bowl of anything in a big casserole dish.

If you take a noticeable amount of food, you have entered a gray area. So you must either replace the "borrowed" item or try to conceal your deed. Resurface the margarine in its tub or smash the corner of the stick so it looks as if it has been dropped instead of cut, add a little

water to the pitcher of orange juice, redistribute the casserole to remove any signs of servings being removed, and your roommates will never suspect you've been in their stash.

Most condiments are up for grabs, so you don't have to worry when borrowing those. But when something is depleted, it can take months before someone finally gives in and replenishes it. Thus, you may have to learn to live without salt, ketchup, or mustard. That's one of the reasons smart single people always pick up a few extra packets of these when they visit fast food restaurants and squirrel them away for a time of condiment famine.

When it comes to KP, two areas seem to create the greatest problems: the sink and the refrigerator. Because conservation is considered a virtue today, you may find you are living with roommates who think it a shame to waste water and soap by washing one measly plate or glass after a meal. Five or fifteen meals later, you will have a sizeable pile of dishes with food residue in varying stages of decomposition. No one person can be blamed for this travesty, and no one will want to tangle with the mess. Thus, a game called Strategy Stacking begins.

You and your roommates must continue adding your cups or saucers to the pile. However, you now proceed with steady hands in order to do so without causing a Melmac avalanche. The stakes increase when you realize there is greasy water hidden in some of the nooks-and-crannies of this free-form sculpture of Teflon and Tupperware.

You know that the game is in its final round when your roommates begin eating all their meals away from home or hiding a clean set of plates and flatware in their rooms and quietly sneaking into the bathroom after each meal to wash them. The breaking point comes when the one with the strongest constitution (also known as the loser) ties a bandana around his face and proceeds to disarm this ptomaine timebomb.

The refrigerator can also harbor culinary timebombs, though the ticking is much quieter. You may go months before finding a once-palatable bowl of fruit salad that has mutated into an alien life-form. Vegetable trays house forgotten produce that have the uncanny abilities to sprout tentacles or puree' themselves at will. And for all you know, Jimmy Hoffa may be in your freezer since everything there falls into one of two categories: items you bought yesterday to cook today or items so camouflaged in aluminum foil, plastic wrap, and frost that you have no idea what these things are or how long they've been freezer burning.

At some point, you and your roommates will jointly get fed up, ditch everything that does not fall into the first category, and throw the icy globs in a dumpster, hoping that they don't find their way back home.

Words of warning about roommates from the # THREE STOOGES

Watch for bowling ball secretly kept on tippy-top shelf of closet.

Never stick head in gas oven when roommate is adjusting the pilot light.

Hire professional wallpaperers—it's less messy and saves you that unpleasant glue aftertaste.

Before roommates help pull your painful, impacted wisdom teeth, ask for references.

Best to wear helmet and goggles when disagreements arise.

When redecorating, it is generally unwise to turn around while carrying a long board through a small room cluttered with ladders and open paint cans.

Be careful walking barefoot in house—someone may have carelessly left anvil or nail-spiked board lying around.

If sleeping on triple-decker beds, do not put the heaviest roommate in top bunk.

For insurance, it is wise to know the differences between baking powder and gun powder.

Do not accept a live wire from roommate while standing in the shower.

MISDEMEANORS

Left refrigerator door open.

Changed the answering machine message you liked.

Left stereo on.

Gets too many after-hours phone calls.

Broke favorite coffee mug.

Left food open in kitchen.

Left dirty dishes in living room.

Took your laundromat quarters.

Failed to clean hair from bathtub drain.

Left clothes in the bathroom.

Tied up telephone for hours.

Invited over rowdy guests.

Played stereo too loud.

FELONIES

Left freezer door open causing meltdown.

Left stove on.

Cooked something that stinks up the place.

Recorded over a TV show you taped.

Acted a little too charming around your date.

"Borrowed" food without replacing it.

Emptied the community candy or cookie jar.

Took your parking space.

Wore your clothes without permission.

Recycled a newspaper clipping you wanted to keep.

Lost TV/VCR/stereo remote control.

CAPITAL OFFENSES

Got pet before discussing it with you.

Invited houseguests without consulting you.

Forgot to give you a phone message.

Started dating your most recent girlfriend/boyfriend.

Finished off your ice cream.

How to oust a ROOMMATE

College Dorm Approach

Wait for your roommate to leave for several hours. Give anonymous phone tip to your landlord that your roommate has an extensive history of smoking in bed and starting fires. Say that the person is also a compulsive liar and will try to deny it if confronted.

Move all his/her belongings into hall or yard. If necessary, solicit help from your friends who never liked him/her anyway or from the person you have lined up to take your current roommate's place. To show that you're really not a thoughtless lout, place a "change of address" kit and a "guide to apartment living" on the top of the stack.

Change the locks and install a burglar alarm. And park your car at a friend's for safe keeping.

Sociopath Approach

In a fit of rage, cite everything the person has ever done that you find offensive. Say you have no idea how many other things he/she has done that have thus far gone undetected. Make the veins on your neck bulge. Pace, rhythmically tapping a rolling pin or bowling trophy against your open palm as you go.

Let your roommate know that lately you've been sneaking over to the firing range for target practice and that makes you think of him/her a lot . . . a lot. Promise to make your roommate's life a never-ending nightmare. Say you've done research and point to the stack of videos that includes *The Hand That Rocks the Cradle, Pacific Heights,* and *Whatever Happened to Baby Jane?* Mention that you've begun a pen pal relationship with Leona Helmsley.

When your roommate runs to pack, collapse from exhaustion and relief.

The Kinder, Gentler Approach

Act nervous and uncomfortable until your roommate asks if there's something wrong. Stammer as you respond, "We need to talk."

Sit down. Look out the window or at the floor. Start off by citing your own shortcomings. Then say, "I know I can be hard to live with." Relate a traumatic episode from childhood which details relational problems (neighborhood kids who wouldn't play with you, a sibling who locked you in a front-loading dryer and made you play "junior astronaut"). Proceed with, "But I can tell you're not . . . well, happy here." When your roommate starts to interrupt you, insist, "Please, let me finish." Choke back a sob.

"I'll only hold you back. I know you need to move on." Recite the lyrics to "Wind Beneath My Wings" followed by "I Will Always Love You."

When your roommate finally manages to protest, "But I don't want to move," quickly respond, "There you go again, thinking of me." Insist that he/she begin packing immediately. And choking back another sob, say, "It's for the best . . . really."

Saturday night, 6:00 P.M.

Stare at phone.

"Don't just sit there. Ring."

"C'mon, ring. I don't want to spend the whole evening just sitting here alone."

Roam around apartment.

"Why do I do this? Why don't I ever make plans?"

Pick up a magazine or cereal box and scan it for something interesting to read. Put it down. Walk back to phone.

"Are you out of order?"

Pick up receiver. Hear dial tone. Feel disappointment. Replace receiver.

"Where is everybody? I wonder if everybody I know is together someplace and they just forgot to invite me."

"What if they didn't forget? What if they just didn't want to invite me? I wonder if I did something to offend one of them."

Stare at phone again.

"What do I care? Those people are all such jerks anyway. Just a bunch of self-involved neurotics."

Roam around apartment. Hear phone ringing in someone else's apartment. Mutter something.

"Well, now what?"

Pick up phone.

"I guess I could call someone."

Draw a blank of who to call.

"It's kinda late. That might be kinda rude. If no one is really at home, I'll be miserable all over again. I'd rather not know."

Hang up phone. Turn on TV. Flip channels incessantly. Find yourself watching a Cher infomercial. Hug a box of Wheat Thins and drink milk from the carton. Fall asleep. Wake up in the middle of the night to find Richard Simmons sweating to the oldies.

"Another forgettable Saturday night."

Go to bed.

The next day, talk to several of your friends who all spent the evening at home alone, watching Cher infomercials, and eating Wheat Thins.

HEALTH CLUB

DOS

Mind if we alternate sets on these weights?

Is this the right way to do this exercise?

DON'TS

Mind if I share your towel?

So what's your target weight?

I love the way the sweat glistens on your forehead.

Would you be able to tell if I pulled my hamstring?

GROCERY

DOS

Have you ever tried this product?

You know, this recipe is going to make way too much for one person.

Hey, would you like a coupon for that? (NOTE: It does require a little extra preparation and a subscription to the Sunday paper but this is your life we're talking about here.)

DON'TS

Mind if I ride in your cart?

What diet products have you found most successful?

Do you think there's more value in two-ply bathroom tissue?

Do you know what's really in bologna?

LAUNDROMAT

DOS

Do you have change for a dollar?

Do you think it would be okay to wash these together?

Is this too full?

DON'TS

Hey, I've got an idea. Let's dry our clothes together.

I love what the fluorescent lights do to your skin tone.

Maybe I'm giddy from the fumes of scented detergents but what's say we fall in love?

Mind if I wash what I'm wearing?

VIDEO STORE

DOS

I'm having a hard time deciding on something. Do you have any suggestions?

Ever feel like you're a Beta format in a VHS world?

Darn, you got the last copy of *(insert name of tape here)*. Don't suppose you'd be interested in watching it together?

DON'TS

Can you believe they haven't released "Three's Company" on video?

Want to go back to my place and rewind?

I don't know about you but I really love comedies. I see enough of that horror stuff down at the mortuary.

Why don't you come over and watch *Batman?* I've got costumes and everything.

If you're planning a hot night out on the town, you must address a few critical questions to avoid getting burned. How will you dress? How will you act? What will you say?

Getting Dolled Up

For women appearance is everything, so allow plenty of time to get ready to go out. Spend a lot of time doing your nails. Remember that there's no such thing as too much eye shadow. Use base the way a dry waller uses spackling. Go for heavy blush; it may be dark where you go so you need that pinkish/reddish/orangeish boost for your cheeks to look naturally healthy. Overaccessorization is a virtue: Wear enough bracelets to sound like a percussionist being mugged, and wear earrings with lots of dangly things so you look like you've stolen the mobiles that hang over a baby's crib.

Fashion Man-euvers

While women become hyperkinetic getting ready for a night on the town, men must work at seeming nonchalant. Practice lowering your heartrate. Learn the fine art of scanning a room without appearing to notice anything until you lock in on a target.

Minimalism is the look in dress for men: Wear pants with the smallest waist possible, and use as few buttons on your shirt as local health laws permit. One key exception to the minimalism rule: Invest in lots of gold jewelry, especially items that can be ordered late at night while watching TV.

The bulk of your time should be spent working on The Hair. Shampoo it, condition it, creme rinse it, mousse it, brush it, fluff it, swoop it, style it, fine-tune it, spray it. Try to make it look as natural as possible.

FEVER
78

If you're going bald, especially work on the swooping. Take hearty strands of hair, hurl them over the top of your head, and let gravity send them cascading down toward the opposite ear. The technique is similar to that used by teenagers to roll someone's trees with toilet paper. If this process is ineffectual or there are stout, changeable winds where you live, consider getting a toupee or hair plugs and possibly a beret or cowboy hat.

The Fine Art of Conversation

Places that offer live music are notoriously loud—deep conversation is not the top priority. So be sure to take time before Saturday night to learn the art of meaningless babble.

Phrases that can be interjected in almost any conversation include "Wow," "Isn't that cute," "Are you kidding me?" "No-o-o-o," "I-love-it," and "That's fan-tastic." You can also easily manage these while staring deeply into the eyes of the person you're talking with and wondering if you turned off the iron.

The Introduction Trap

The only thing tougher than meeting new people is remembering the names of people you've already met. If you are at a loss for someone's name, look pleasantly surprised when he/she greets you, smile brightly, and say, "How *are* you? It's *so* good to see you." This will probably get you off the hook unless you need to introduce the mystery person to friends whose names you still remember. In this case, try to signal your friends to introduce themselves.

An easy method when you're stuck is to pull your known friend closer into your circle, and start with the names you know: "Phyllis,

George, have you guys met?" Shoot a desparate stare at Phyllis and George that says, *Help me out here.* If your friends have ever been in your shoes, they should give you the necessary reinforcement.

Making Your Exit

Burt Bacharach and Hal David were right: "Knowing when to leave can be the smartest thing that anyone can learn."

Make your exit while activities are at their peak. If you do, people will perceive you as the life of the party. And later, they will tell you that "things went downhill after you left." If you have established yourself over the years as part of this "singles scene" and have sufficiently worked the crowd this evening, your departure should be reminiscent of the scene in *The Sound of Music* when the townspeople bid the Von Trapp children good night.

Lively, little divorced white female, wannabe grandma, likes people and parties, slightly blonde, seeking knowledgeable, literate, active, expressive, funny man of originality, with washing machine. Non-smoker. Please send photo of washing machine.

At last, the Maytag repairman won't be the loneliest man in town.

Super computer having overcome original programming, wishes to study human life as a participant. Having obtained an attractive biological unit of 33 years, desires to share data, explore and exchange info on such experiences as recreation, romance, love and family.

If this man isn't a Trekkie, he's missing the opportunity of a lifetime.

Classy lady looking for a sincere, thoughtful, honest Caucasian gentleman.

Rule of thumb: anyone who uses describes herself as classy probably isn't.

Magical, Mystical, Elegant, Creative, Empathetic, Intense, Sensitive, Psychic, Brilliant, Warm, Off-the-Wall, Voluptuous.

Attention, Doug Henning, your dream girl has just beamed down!

Would like to meet a gentleman who is happy with who they are.

All schizophrenics, here's just what you (and you and you) have been looking for.

SWM, Master of Martial Arts & Oriental Massage, world traveler, likes bowling photography and walks.

Is this guy unique or what? I mean, how many world traveling kung fu massage masters like bowling—much less bowling photography?

VERY CREATIVE MAN, 36 working on global reform project. Living way ahead of my time. Open for new co-creative relationships.

> If you're reforming the whole globe, do you think you've really got time for a co-creative relationship?

RUSSIAN LADY, 41, 5'4", 130 lbs., poor, intelligent, professional, seeks husband.

> Wait, isn't this the storyline from *Fiddler on the Roof?*

SOUTHERN BELLE seeks Rhett Butler—30, attractive, fun-loving, sincere lady seeks Jewish, handsome, professional, humorous, physically fit guy, 28–37.

> Since when is Rhett a mensch?

SWM, 28—Music business professional, successful and reputedly extremely handsome seeking single female, 22–30, who has no immediate child-rearing ambitions. Should be non-Republican, slender, and a music lover.

> If you're looking for someone slender you might want to reconsider a Republican. It's looks like they'll be experiencing lean years until at least 1996.

ALGERIAN YOUNG MAN—35 years old, single, mysterious, very rare quality, very sensible, rich in many sciences and secrets, would like to meet lovely girls, nice with high qualities from all over the world. All ages are allowed.

> Maybe all ages are allowed in Algeria but you could find yourself rich in the many sciences and secrets of a cellblock if you're not very sensible.

Jack and Jill

Jack and Jill went up the hill

To fetch a pail of water;

But Jack wasn't ready to commit,

Causing Jill to throw a fit,

And they both sought counseling after.

Peter, Peter

Peter, Peter, pumpkin-eater,

Had a wife and couldn't keep her;

Now he lives on stale baloney

'Cause he's in deep for alimony.

Little Miss Muffet

Little Miss Muffet

Sat on her tuffet,

Eating her curds and whey.

No guy ever called her

With plans to forestall her

From just watching TV all day.

Sing a Song of Singleness

Sing a song of singleness,

Poor lonely guy,

Surviving every day

On frozen pot pie.

When the pie is opened,

He reflects upon his life,

Holds his breath, takes a bite,

Thinks, "I've got to find a wife."

Hickory Dickory, Doc

Hickory dickory, Doc,

Can you stop my biological clock?

Romance hit the skids,

But I'm still wanting kids.

Hickory dickory . . . Doc!

Yankee Doodle

Yankee Doodle went to London,

Riding on a pony;

Spent his time on horsin' 'round

Instead of matrimony.

Yankee Doodle, keep it up.

You think you're such a dandy.

When mid-life crisis kicks your can,

Best keep your toupee handy.

Humpty Dumpty

Humpty Dumpty sat on a wall.

Humpty Dumpty had a great fall.

His girl didn't like him and she found another.

In therapy, they traced it all back to his mother.

Mary Had a Little Lamb

Mary had a little lamb.

She'd rather have a man.

Everywhere that Mary went,

She revealed her plan.

One day in a fit of rage,

She hit the panic button.

Now she has no man or lamb,

But lots and lots of mutton.

If Wishes Were Horses

If wishes were horses, beggars would ride.

If turnips were watches, I would wear one by my side.

And if girls with the blues

Could trade them for "I do's",

It'd sure boost the sales of *Modern Bride.*

Mary, Mary

Mary, Mary, quite contrary,

How will you ever wed?

Your demands are alarming;

There is no Prince Charming.

Will you settle for Al Bundy instead?

How to attend a WEDDING

As a general rule, single people do not enjoy attending weddings. However, you can only use the "I think I'm coming down with something" excuse so many times until you must finally attend a friend's nuptial festivities. When you are roped into watching someone tie the knot, here are some guidelines to follow.

Women

Go with a small covey of single women so you won't be so obvious and will have someone to review the wedding with later. Mentally critique the decorations, bridesmaids' dresses, and music. As the bride comes down the aisle, notice how much weight she has lost. Remind yourself that you absolutely must lose a few pounds.

During slower sections, fantasize what your own ideal wedding would be like. Incorporate Disneyesque elements into your dream, like animated birds holding up the train of your wedding dress. Snap back to reality. Then decide the Disney scene was more interesting and return there.

At the pronouncement, visualize your face replacing the bride's. Let tears form in your eyes. And smile at your friends the way the nuns smiled at one another at the end of Maria's wedding in *The Sound of Music*.

If you choose to go to the reception, try not to be among the first to arrive. You will stand out. Instead, time things so that you can be on the back end of the first wave of guests.

Engage in meaningless conversation with others as you enter. When someone asks if this isn't a wonderful occasion, try not to say, "I couldn't be happier," because you know that you could—if you were in that wedding dress, you definitely could be happier.

WEDDING
96

Try to find an inobtrusive place to sit with friends and hold your ground until you can congratulate the happy couple and get out of there. When the bride says something like "I guess you're next," suppress the desire to shove her head into the cake and demurely say "Oh, I don't know." If the photographer rounds you up for the tossing of the bouquet, clench your teeth, and hiss to a friend, "Rather cruel little tradition, don't you think?"

When the bouquet is thrown, remember only women under twenty-five are allowed to really reach for it. Women over twenty-five tend to like to push other people forward, thus blocking themselves from the camera's view and ensuring that they don't have to worry about the razzing that follows catching the cursed thing.

If the wedding requires you to throw rice for the couple's exit, throw half-heartedly, and then retire to one of your friends' apartments where you will take off your shoes, rub your feet, and recap the high and low points of the affair.

Men

If you are not preparing to propose to the woman you are dating, do not go with her to the wedding—the pressure is just too great. Go by yourself and scope out the crowd. Make a beeline for one of the coveys of women so you can be instantly transformed from a cowardly loner to a virile stud-muffin.

As the wedding party enters the sanctuary, study the groomsmen and wonder how much it costs to rent a tux these days. Notice the bridesmaids. Squint your eyes, trying to see if any are wearing wedding bands, and thus if there is any point in introducing yourself at the reception.

Think about what kind of music you would choose for a wedding—not necessarily your own. Think about all the dorky songs you've heard played at weddings. Suppress a snicker. Play with the wedding program, hymnals in the bookrack, or any other "toys" available.

Survey the crowd for other single guys. Notice some are slouching or are wearing ill-fitting suits. Sit up straight and adjust your clothes. Pull several times on your cuffs, using this opportunity to check your watch and see how long the ceremony is taking. Wonder what kind of food they're having at the reception. At the pronouncement, mentally sing a chorus of "Another One Bites the Dust." Press toward the center aisle so you can make a quick exit for the reception after the wedding party has recessed.

Be among the first to get to the reception and scope out the food.

To avoid being perceived as a pig, don't be the first person in line. If you're third or fourth, you'll still get your shot at everything before it gets picked over. Also, if you eat quickly, you'll be able to get back in line with an entirely different group of people, start from scratch, and not have to worry about making dinner.

Because you made the bride and groom take such a beating on the food and drink tab, you owe it to the honored couple to wish them well. If they suggest that your time for marriage ought to be approaching, chuckle half-heartedly and change subjects—ask when they're going to cut the cake.

If the wedding photographer tries to get all the single men to line up to catch the garter, do so begrudgingly. When the groom fires the garter, don't even flinch a muscle. Let the inexperienced guys grovel, and notice how the single women are taking note who seems to be anxious about getting married.

The formalities over, the couple will finally make their exit. If you're sending them off in a shower of birdseed, throw overhand. Ignore the possibility that you might put an eye out. If the groom or bride are really good friends, decorate the car before they leave the reception, writing double entendres in soap or shoe polish all over it.

Admire your handiwork as the car speeds away. Then reach in your pocket, grab a handful of dry-roasted peanuts you scarfed from the food table, and saunter to your car.

If you don't stay in close contact with former classmates, you have carte blanche to create revisionist history at your reunion. Depending upon your intentions, you can evoke awe or empathy from your peers.

Heart on Your Sleeve/Head on Their Shoulder

If you want to gain the consolation of someone for the evening, use an angst-filled tale of unrequited love and tragedy. Borrow liberally from *Love Story* or *Ghost,* but try to add a twist that makes the story yours. Don't directly follow the storyline of any made-for-television "disease of the week" movie, because people who are likely to believe your story probably watch those. Maintain victim status throughout the tale.

Ask if there's someplace quieter you could go to talk. Mention how hard it was to summon the courage to come to the reunion but you really wanted to see those few people who, by simply thinking of them, had given you the strength to go on. Stammer and say, "Would you hold me?"

Leech as much emotional support as possible from as many

people as possible, but make sure you've made your getaway before your classmates start comparing notes on their encounters with you.

How to Be Successful Without Really Trying

Wear a fake wedding band and repeatedly say how sorry you are that your spouse couldn't make it because he/she would love to meet your old friends. Unfortunately he/she is: a) closing a deal on a private Caribbean island, b) on a top-secret initiative in the Middle East, or c) running a halfway house for former child stars and there was trouble on the "Different Strokes" wing. Depending upon the gullibility of your friends, it may be possible to use a combination of stories.

If desired, you can say you have children but it is suggested that, in order to make your lifestory more plausible, you should include at least one heart-rending, semi-tragic note. For example, "The toddler failed to make the cut in MIT's pre-school program, but we're going to get little Shannon a tutor and try again next year."

Relational problems of singles portrayed on "GILLIGAN'S ISLAND"

An example of television programming at its finest, "Gilligan's Island" offers contemporary society an anthropological study of single people.

Gilligan

A prime example of Peter Pan Syndrome, he refused to grow up and was unwilling to commit to anything that took longer than building a hut.

Skipper

His sense of failure in losing the SS *Minnow* shipwrecked his belief that he was able to carry through with anything meaningful, thus he never could commit to a lasting relationship.

Professor

Secure only in his career, he deferred relationships to concentrate on his studies of hydroelectric power, solar energy, and the amazing versatility of coconut shells. Instead of being called by his given name, he hid behind his academic title which allowed him to distance himself from others.

Ginger

Instead of cultivating her inner beauty, she poured herself into evening gowns (which look just a tad out of place on a three-hour cruise). Her concentration on physical appearance made her the kind of girl who got offers, not proposals.

Mary Ann

Sure she was cute, enthusiastic, and made a great coconut cream pie. But she was just too gosh-darn swell to generate genuine passion. Men would feel as if they were dating their sister. Had she been asked out, it certainly wouldn't have lasted because she was bound to have a group of similar friends who would be quick to say that no man was really good enough for someone as swell as she.

Problems associated with being a single U.S. PRESIDENT

First family portrait in White House looks a little empty alongside predecessors.

Dates covered live on C-SPAN.

Speech writers come up with really corny pick-up lines.

Sam Donaldson always wiggling his eyebrows to take babes away from you.

Hounded at press conference the morning after a date by reporters shouting, "Didja kiss her? Didja kiss her?"

Dates want to know when you're going to settle down and get a real job.

Tricky prenuptial agreement: "Who gets the House?" Also, "Who gets the Senate?"

Proposals from high-ranking Russian babes on Kremlin hotline scheming to get their green cards.

Old college buddies wanting to borrow Air Force One to impress their girlfriends.

Unfair pressure from Supreme Court justices saying, "I've got a granddaughter who wants to marry a President."

Cynical press aides refer to your date as "First Lady of the Evening."

Senators want to give you dating advice.

Mood is broken every time you and your date get out of the limo and the marching band strikes up "Hail to the Chief."

Date reaches in purse for lipstick and Secret Service wrestles her to the ground.

Because single men and women often spend time together without defining the terms of their relationship, they can often share each other's company without ever knowing for sure what's going on between them. Realize that what you may consider a date may be viewed by your partner as just hanging out. The following guidelines will help you determine if what you did was a date. If you answer yes to more than twelve questions, surprise and congratulations! You were on a date.

General Questions

Were you nervous?

Did you set your plans more than two days in advance?

Did you tell your friends you were going out on a date?

Did your friends tell you they had heard you were going out on a date?

Did you make a lot of eye contact while you were out together?

Did you purposely avoid talking about other people you had dated?

Did you kiss? If not, did you want to?

Women

Did you shave your legs?

Did you buy a new outfit? (double points for this one)

Did you have horrendous problems with your hair?

Was he dressed nicely?

Did he pay?

Did he have a clear-cut plan for the evening?

Did he open doors and perform other gentlemanly acts?

Did he walk you to your door?

Did he say he would call again?

Did he call again within forty-eight hours?

Men

Did you rehearse any part of the conversation beforehand?

Did you clean out your car?

Did you wax your car? (double points for this one)

Did you iron anything you wore?

Did you shave right before you picked her up?

Did she ask that they leave the onions off her dinner selection?

Did she touch your arm when you talked?

If you went to a movie, did you share the armrest?

When you took her home, did she say how much she enjoyed herself?

Did she invite you in?

Success in relationships depends upon correctly analyzing the data provided. When you hear the following leading indicators, it is safe to assume that your future together looks promising.

My dog seems to like you.

I've got these two tickets and I hate to go alone.

Want to practice the fireman's carry?

Boy, my shoulders are really tight.

You know, I've never kissed a guy with a moustache.

Airfares are so high I don't think I can afford to go home for Thanksgiving.

If you scratch my back, I'll scratch yours.

Does it seem kinda cold in here to you?

You know, I've never kissed a girl with a moustache (must be used with discretion).

Could you teach me mouth-to-mouth resuscitation?

I want to know what love is. I want you to show me.

He says: I'll call you.

> He means: within the next week.
>
> She thinks: tomorrow.

He says: Would you want to maybe get together sometime?

> He means: Would you say yes if I asked you out?
>
> She thinks: Is this a date or a 'friend thing'?

He says: Do you have plans Friday night?

> He means: Is your schedule clear for me to ask you out?
>
> She thinks: If I say yes, am I discouraging him and if I say no do I sound like I'm a loser?

He says: Do you like football?

> He means: Would you like to go to a football game? OR
>
> Is this a woman who will let me hang out with my football buddies if we start dating?

She thinks: If I don't go along with this, I'll be a widow on game
day.

He says: Where would you like to go?

He means: I value your opinions and wishes. OR

I didn't plan ahead. You got any ideas?

She thinks: Oh great, another spineless, indecisive man. OR

He doesn't even think enough of me to plan a date.

He says: Let's just be friends.

He means: You're wearing me out. I need space. OR

I've found somebody else. OR

You annoy me but I don't want to tell you the truth.

She thinks: There's another woman. OR

Why do I always date jerks?

She says, she means, # HE THINKS

She says: My folks are coming to town this weekend.

> She means: Is this relationship serious enough that you would want to meet them? OR
>
> If you really care about me, you won't make me face them alone.

> He thinks: Yikes! She thinks I'm about to propose.

She says: Want to do something after work?

> She means: I'm interested in you. OR
>
> There's a rumor going around the office and I want to find out if it's true. OR
>
> My friends are ragging me about never initiating relationships and this will get them off my back.

> He thinks: Is she asking me out?

She says: It's fun to go to weddings with you.

> She means: I've got a wedding coming up and I need an escort. OR
> You are good company.

> He thinks: She's thinking that if we have a good time attending
> weddings, then we'd make a great bride and groom.

She says: Do you know anything about cars?

> She means: Can you keep me from getting ripped off by the car
> sales or repair people?

> He thinks: She needs me. This is great! OR
> She needs me. I can't handle the pressure.

She says: What are you looking for in a relationship?

> She means: Are you going to steal my heart and walk away? OR
> You're confusing the heck out of me. OR
> Can we call this a relationship?

> He thinks: Is there a right answer here?

She says: Let me get this one (meaning: pay for the meal).

She means: I don't want to be perceived as a sponge. OR

Don't treat me as financially inferior. OR

I like this relationship and this is my way of saying so.

He thinks: She's giving me a slow brush-off. OR

She thinks I'm not capable of providing for her. OR

She wants to take control of the relationship.

She says: Let's just be friends.

She means: Let's just be friends (this may be the only time she

means exactly what she says). OR

You kiss like a fish. OR

Someone else churns my butter.

He thinks: I blew it. I've failed again.

12 STEPS of dating recovery

1. We admitted that we were powerless over our date lives and that they had become unmanageable.

2. We came to believe that, because we had made such a mess of our dating lives since seventh grade, a power greater than ourselves was needed to help us. (After taking a good look at the Amway organization, we decided we needed something even stronger.)

3. We made a decision to turn our calendar and our Friday nights over to the care of Matchmakers International or the lady at work who wants to fix us up with someone she knows.

4. We made a searching inventory of ourselves so as not to spend the rest of our lives married to someone who we might claim caused the ruin of our lives.

5. We admitted to God, ourselves, and to another human being the desire to return to arranged marriages so we could avoid the anguish of dating. Perhaps someday when we're stronger we will make the same admission to our parents.

6. We were entirely ready to have the guts to risk life with another person by committing to the possibility of marriage.

7. We humbly asked our dates to overlook our shortcomings, acknowledging that on a graded scale we lie somewhere between God's gift to the opposite sex and a mere fluke of the universe.

8. We made a list of all persons we had strung along and then dumped and are willing to face them and make amends (although we'd rather just send them Christmas cards).

9. We made direct amends to such people wherever possible except when to do so would injure them or put our lives on the "ABC Sunday Night Movie."

10. We continued to take personal inventory. When we were aware that our expectations of a date/mate were beyond the realm of possibility, we would humbly admit it and remember Roseanne are closer to reality than June Cleaver.

11. We sought through prayer and meditation to discover the true meaning of such phrases as "I need some space," "I can't wait around forever," and "The ball's in your court."

12. Having had a spiritual awakening as a result of these steps and having watched *When Harry Met Sally* enough to memorize entire scenes, we tried to carry this message of recovery to our single friends who had just about had it up to there with all our whining about being single.

Other than getting a complete physical or trying on swimsuits, few things are more unsettling than dating—and especially the first date. So many things can go wrong. He can show up early when you're running fifteen minutes late. He sees your roommate and seems more attracted to her than to you. You dress for a nice evening, and he wears jeans with a ripped-out knee. You check your answering machine while he's in the room and your best friend has called to ask if he's a good kisser. After he leaves, you discover a sesame seed stuck between your front teeth.

If you're lucky, he'll remember the things that went right. Yes, you were late getting ready but you looked like someone he could be proud to be seen with. Over dinner, the conversation was easy and pleasant (and you managed to slip in something about your roommate's fiancé).

The difference in dress was a little awkward at first, but it provided an opportunity to talk about how we too often emphasize the things that really don't matter.

Hearing the answering machine message, he asks if you need information to file a report and kisses you. And when he arrives to pick you up for your next date, he brings a box of sesame seeds instead of a bouquet of flowers.

HOLY TERRORS of church singles groups

Watch for reformed lounge lizards who've traded "What's your sign?" for "What's your favorite Bible verse?"

The possibility always exists that someone will walk up to you and say, "God told me that you're supposed to marry me" (get suspicious if you hear them say that to three other people).

People frequently tell the story of the animals entering the ark two-by-two to encourage relationships.

Because "it is better to marry than to burn" (1 Corinthians 7:9), be on the lookout for people who could spontaneously combust.

All unspoken prayer requests are assumed to concern something sexual.

At church, you must remember that "a little black book" refers to a pocket Bible.

People who join hands with you for prayer sometimes don't want to let go.

Because abstinence makes the heart grow fonder, be aware that some people may be absolutely eat up with fondness.

Beware of those who push the limits of "greet one another with a holy kiss" (Romans 16:16).

How BONANZA would be different if Ben Cartwright remarried

Ponderosa's hacienda look replaced by lots of frilly things.

Ben shoots Sherriff Coffey after one-too-many "she's got you wrapped around her little finger" jibes.

Little Joe warned about leaving hair in basin.

Hop Sing forced to cut crust off bread of watercress sandwiches.

Hop Sing forced to find out what watercress is.

Ben told to give the leather vest a rest.

Hoss not allowed to say "dadburn it" because a lady is present.

No more sitting around fireplace in skivvies.

Victoria Barkley from "Big Valley" invited over for bridge every Thursday.

If Ben's wife had three very lovely girls, it would've opened opportunity for a pioneer version of "The Brady Bunch."

SONGS singles hate to hear

"The Worst That Could Happen"/Brooklyn Bridge

A recurring scenario in contemporary music goes something like this: boy meets girl; boy likes girl; girl likes boy; girl breaks up with boy; boy falls apart. In this song, the additional kicker is that the girl gets engaged to someone else—a saga that has probably sent more than one young man into therapy.

"Alone Again Naturally"/Gilbert O'Sullivan

Another poor guy gets left at the altar, then contemplates suicide. Enough already!

"I Never Will Marry"/Linda Ronstadt

The female equivalent to the girl leaves boy song, though in this song, the boy leaves on a train, which provides a little folksy dignity.

"One Is the Loneliest Number"/Three Dog Night

If this song doesn't make you want to subscribe to *Alaska Men* or send for an Asian mail-order bride, nothing will.

"Everybody Has a Hungry Heart"/Bruce Springsteen

So we share this problem. Is that supposed to make me feel better?

"To All the Girls I've Loved Before"/Julio Iglesias & Willie Nelson

Who made Captain Mantan and the King of Braided Hair God's gifts to women? And why do nice guys have to bear the heat for their pompousness just because there's a chromosonal resemblance?

"The Wedding Song"/Noel Paul Stookey

The older you get, the longer the song seems.

No healthy person would want the neglect I have to offer.

Jerry Seinfeld

Marriage is a wonderful invention, but then again, so is the bicycle repair kit.

Billy Connolly, Scottish comedian

Marriage is a great institution, but I'm not ready for an institution yet.

Mae West

If men knew how women pass their time when they're alone, they'd never marry.

O. Henry

I want to be alone.

Greta Garbo, in *Grand Hotel*

I don't want to be alone. I want to be left alone.

Katharine Hepburn

Girls who wear zippers shouldn't live alone.

John W. Van Druten

Women over 30 are at their best, but men over 30 are too old to recognize it.

Jean-Paul Belmondo, French film star

Every woman needs a man to discover her.

Charlie Chaplin

A gentleman is a patient wolf.

Henrietta Tiarks, British socialite

I've sometimes thought of marrying and then I've thought again.

Noel Coward

It's a woman's business to get married as soon as possible and a man's to keep unmarried as long as he can.

George Bernard Shaw

A man in love is incomplete until he has married. Then he's finished.

Zsa Zsa Gabor

If there's anything worse than a woman living alone, it's a woman saying she likes it.

Thelma Ritter, in *Pillow Talk*

I'm very glad and grateful that my profession will make me a useful, happy, and independent spinster.

Louisa May Alcott

He who is without a wife dwells without blessing, life, joy, help, good, and peace—and without defense against temptation.

Talmud

When a bachelor dies, girls are avenged.

Zohar

Glitches in marriage VIRTUAL REALITY experience

Instead of actually entering into holy matrimony, futurists tell us we may be able to experience marriage through a technological wonder called virtual reality. Presently, however, there are a few things amiss in this scientific simulation of wedded bliss.

Mr. and Ms. PacMan make annoying next-door neighbors.

Can't stop hackers from spying on you.

Husbands sound like Homer Simpson; wives, like 411 operator recording.

Can't cut off endless loop of Jetsons theme song.

Men tend to look like Mario Brothers.

Dr. Smith from "Lost in Space" keeps showing up at inopportune times to look for "that ridiculous robot."

The experience always starts with wedding plans but resets before the honeymoon causing considerable frustration.

Women tend to look like Mario Brothers.

At wedding, the HAL computer sings "Daisy, Daisy."

Silhouettes of the two robots and guy from "Mystery Science Theatre 2000" appear in lower right corner of field of vision and make snide remarks.

Inlaws can spit fire.

Ways to MOCK your married friends

Make a patchwork quilt of all the things you did together when you were both single.

Tell them how much more comfortable and restful it is sleeping single in a double bed.

Unexpectedly call the same-sex spouse, invite him/her to do something fun that would require immediate response, then say, "Oh, I forgot. You're married."

Start fights between spouses by mentioning a previous relationship one of the spouses had before they got married.

Plan a party exclusively for single people and mention to your couple friends how great it's going to be. Then add, "You probably wouldn't want to come because it's going to be all single people."

Eat all your meals in restaurants, flaunting that you can afford such a luxury because you don't have to save for the education of future children.

Slip in subliminal suggestions such as, "You're going to forget your anniversary."

INSIGHTS on singleness from the Mary Tyler Moore show

If you're going to be at home by yourself, it helps to have a cool apartment (preferably in an old house).

You can't leave piles of dirty laundry lying around when your living room is also your bedroom.

Nerdy guys will be drawn to you; normal guys will cause you to do something goofy.

You don't look as inept if you have a wacky and desperate single neighbor.

Sue Ann Syndrome: celibacy looks much more appealing in the context of an aging vamp.

When you're single, you're free to buy all the scarves and pantsuits you want.

You walk really erect on park sidewalks when you wear platform shoes.

Well-meaning married co-workers will treat you as a charity case; rebuff their pity by being darn perky.

When you're single, you're free to stop in the middle of the street and throw your cap into the air anytime you want.

Over time, you become a stronger person by having to learn to deal with theme song which proclaims, "Girl, this time you're all alone."

Selected GREETING CARDS from the new singles collection

Happy Birthday from your therapist.

Good News! Due to increased life spans, you won't be an old maid for another 20 years.

From both of us to the one of you.

Happy Independence Day! It's as close as you single people get to your own national holiday.

Hope you're having a swell Valentine's Day. If not, call 1–800-CRISIS. Trained phone counselors are standing by.

New Year's Greetings from your accountant. Will this be your year for joint-return magic?

You've got the flu and you're single. But look on the bright side. At least one of your troubles will be over in 24 hours.

Congratulations on your promotion! At least your professional life is moving forward.

ADVANTAGES **to being single**

Allows extra car seats to be used as filing cabinets or lockers.

Speed through express check-out in grocery while families look like competitors on Supermarket Sweep.

No wrestling over organization of closet space.

Maintain autonomy over the checkbook.

Faster seating in restaurants.

No expenditures for marriage counseling.

GLOSSARY **from the single file**

aftershockabsorber—(af-tur-shok-ab-zor-bur) the person you date after you've been dumped. Also, called a *reboundee*.

allmanac—(awl-man-ak) the woman who generates an irresistible attraction from males.

altarcall-waiting—(awl-tur-kawl way-ting) the bachelor who takes sudden detours just when it seems inevitable that he'll finally walk down the aisle.

bachalaureate—(batch-uh-law-re-ut) the send-off speech given by single guys when one of their number is getting married.

balkano—(bawlk-ay-no) fight that erupts when participants in a blind date meet and one person decides it would be better to sit home and dig change out of the sofa cushions than to go out together.

blocketeer—(blok-it-teer) roommate who thoughtlessly stands in front of the TV so no one else can see.

bouchaos—(boo-kay-os) mad scramble for the bouquet thrown by the bride; considered a harmless tradition if you're 20 but a device of public ridicule if you're 35.

bunter—(bunt-ur) polite but brief chit-chat with someone you have recently stopped dating.

chatastrophe—(chat-az-tro-fe) a get-to-know-someone-better conversation which starts to go wrong and keeps going.

convention—-(cahn-ven-shun) a large gathering of nuns, or figuratively, single women.

counterfit—(kownt-ur-fit) the tantrum thrown when you realize that your roommate has left dirty dishes stacked on every horizontal plane in the kitchen.

cupidity—(kew-pid-it-tee) being foolishly, helplessly, hopelessly in love with someone who doesn't even know you exist.

.

dateaholic—(date-uh-hol-ik) the person who packs his or her social calendar tighter than a can of Vienna sausages.

dateline—(date-line) pitch used to get someone to go out with you.

defoxification—(de-fox-if-uh-ka-shun) a man's image of a woman shattered by seeing her without her hair done or her make-up on.

domiciliation—(dom-uh-silh-ee-ay-shun) bringing an end to roommate wars.

dude magnet—(dood mag-net) any possession that attracts men: tennis dresses, nice stereos, and big friendly dogs are dude magnets. A subscription to *Soap Opera* Digest, a pack of cigarettes rolled up in the sleeve of the blouse, and press-on nails are not.

eggspiration date—(eg-spur-ay-shun dayt) the day the biological clock stops ticking; the approach of this date often sends women out with marginally desirable men who can be hammered into husband/father material.

excues—(eks-kews) hints from your former steady date that there's a possibility of getting back together.

extacy—(ex-ta-see) the elation you feel when you see an old love interest and realize you're overjoyed that you're out of that relationship.

fabricabrac—(fab-brik-uh-brak) that favorite old sweatshirt your roommate found lying around and turned into rags to clean his or her car.

fix-you-upper—(fiks-yew-up-pur) a modern-day matchmaker.

gemitation—(jem-it-ta-shun) the "rock" which you thought was the real thing until it changed colors when you washed your hands.

hergatory—(hur-ga-tor-ee) time a man spends being punished for falling short of a woman's expectations, as shown in the following conversation:

> He: Why won't you talk to me? What'd I do?
>
> She: You know perfectly well what you did.
>
> He: No, really, I don't.
>
> She: Well, until you're willing to apologize, I don't want you to call me.

hisitation—(hiz-uh-ta-shun) that awkward moment before he leans over and kisses her good night.

histerics—(hiz-ter-iks) when a man goes crazy over a cherished possession which he feels has been misused or mistreated:

> He: Are you nuts?! What are you doing using my nine iron to prop the door open? That's a graphite shaft you've used like a broom handle. . . . No, just forget it. It's fine. . . . Just fine. Might as well just drive a stake through my heart.

hypeochondria—(hype-o-kon-dre-ah) the fear that once again your friends have exaggerated the information concerning your blind date, elevating a store clerk at Radio Shack to a consultant with an international computer brokerage.

insecurity guard—(in-se-kure-it-tee gard) other people in the house who threaten your privacy with your date.

indullgents—(in-dul-jents) those brainy guys who don't have a chance when women are interested only in physical appearance but become more attractive when ladies switch their focus from the size of a guy's pectorials to the size of his portfolio.

keptomaniac—(kep-toe-mane-ee-ak) the roommate with the annoying habit of borrowing things that never get returned.

maidenformula—(may-den-form-you-la) the curse that determines that some women will be "always a bridesmaid, never a bride."

malebail—(mayl-bayl) when a woman ditches plans with other women because a guy asks her out. Also known as sorority rule.

manorabilia—(man-or-uh-be-le-uh) ticket stubs, restaurant matches, and other items kept by a woman to remind her of a meaningful date.

mantagonist—(man-tag-oh-nist) a woman angry at men because she has been burned so many times she wears aloe vera lotion instead of lip gloss.

marital status quo—(meyr-it-tul stat-us kwo) still unmarried.

meateorite—(meet-ee-or-ite) the otherworldly foodlike substance found living in your refrigerator months after it originally landed there.

mendorsement—(men-dors-ment) approval of the girl you're dating by the guys you hang out with.

missage—(mis-ej) the phone call your roommate forgot to tell you about.

missplace—(mis-place) dwelling where several women live.

nerdaway—(nurd-uh-way) a fake wedding band, which can be quickly removed if someone interesting appears.

notorious—(no-tor-ee-us) the woman who has gained a reputation for turning down dates like Howard Johnson turns down sheets.

pairanoia—(pare-uh-noy-ya) overwhelming dread of being someplace where there will be only couples and you.

pairasite—(pare-uh-site) place where pairanoia occurs.

partyner—(par-te-nur) the longsuffering opposite-sex person you always call upon when you have to have a date for company functions, weddings, etc.

pasta la vista—(pah-stah la vees-ta) the "dear John" dinner featured in the singles' cookbook *Microwaving Goodbye.*

petal attraction—(pet-tul uh-trak-shun) the technique used by men when trying to absolve themselves of guilt, which posits that even if she hates me, maybe she'll like the flowers.

postmate—(post-mayt) your non-existent spouse, e.g., Mrs. M. T. Arms, who frequently receives junk mail.

proxysemics—(prox-see-sem-iks) the natural law of geography espoused by married people, stating that single people who live close to each other or work in the same office should make a great couple.

randomonium—(ran-dum-moan-nee-um) illogical process of picking an object of affection without experiencing any genuine attraction.

rotoroommate—(rote-toe-room-mate) the dislodging of an undesirable person living with you.

scornucopia—(skorn-you-cope-ee-uh) ill will generated from your ex's friends after the break-up.

shundance—(shun-dance) tactfully sidestepping advances from an undesirable suitor by using your roommate to screen calls.

shunburn—(shun-burn) the firm no you give the undesirable suitor, once you toss tact to the wind and after your roommate gets tired of being a human shield.

solojourners—(so-lo-jurn-urs) people who vacation alone.

solows—(so-lows) depressed condition caused by being alone too long that makes you want to climb into bed under fifty pounds of blankets, eat ice cream until you can't breathe, and watch TV talk shows until you find someone whose life looks more hopeless than yours.

stoperator—(stop-ur-rate-ur) the roommate you have to have a meaningless little phone conversation with before you can talk to your boyfriend/girlfriend.

subtitling—(sub-tite-ul-ing) a written exercise for women to practice substituting their current name with the possibilities that lie ahead in marriage, i.e., Mrs. John Hines, Karen Hines, Karen Duncan-Hines.

thermonuclear war—(thur-mo-nu-klee-ur war) battle between roommates over the appropriate temperature setting.

towery—(tow-ur-ee) a dowry that's really stacked up through the years making the prospective bride not only a real find but a quick way to raise a guy's standard of living.

tumblewad—(tum-bul-wahd) dust bunnies and hair balls which gather under your roommate's bed and make their way into the hallway just before your guests arrive.

ultimatem—(ul-tum-ay-tum) throwing down the gauntlet with the choice of getting married or getting lost.

wellwillhewinkie—(well-wil-he-wink-ee) puzzling question queried at a social gathering by a woman who is giving all the inviting signs she knows to get a guy to flirt with her.

womaniac—(wo-mane-ee-ak) a fellow who feels alarmed at social functions without a woman on his arm.

wreconomist—(rek-con-oh-mist) roommate who replaces something he/she borrowed with an inferior brand under the theory "they're all alike and this one was cheaper."

wreckconciliation—(rek-kon-sil-ee-ay-shun) a specific form of domiciliation, this truce is necessary after a roommate has trashed the apartment or house and done nothing to restore order.

BIBLIOGRAPHY

1. *Inside America*. Louis Harris. Vintage. 1987.
2. "Back to the Nest." *The Tennessean*. January 24, 1993, p.1F.
3. *Statistical Abstract of the United States*. Bureau of the Census. US Department of Commerce 1987.
4. *The Harper's Index*. Lewis Lapham, Michael Polllan, Eric Etheridge. Henry Holt. 1987.
5. Public Opinion. May/June 1987.
6. *What Are The Chances?*. Bernard Siskin, Jerome Staller, David Rorvik, Crown Publishers, Inc. 1989.
7. *The 1985 Virginia Slims American Women's Opinion Poll*. The Roper Organization, Inc. 1985.
8. *What Are The Chances?*. Bernard Siskin, Jerome Staller, David Rorvik, Crown Publishers, Inc. 1989.
9. *Statistical Abstract of the United States*. Bureau of the Census. US Department of Commerce 1987.
10. "What Americans Fear." Louis Harris and Associates, Inc. 1993.

11. "Public Attitudes Toward Risk." Louis Harris and Associates, Inc. Conducted for The Insurance Information Institute. 1983.
12. *Inside America*. Louis Harris. Vintage. 1987.
13. *Statistical Abstract of the United States*. Bureau of the Census. US Department of Commerce 1987.
14. *Report to the Nation on Crime and Justice*. US Department of Justice. 1983.
15. "What Americans Fear." Louis Harris and Associates, Inc. 1993.
16. "The American Male Opinion Index." *Gentleman's Quarterly*. 1988.